INJUSTICE
GODS AMONG US

VOLUME 1

THIS STORY TAKES PLACE BEFORE
THE START OF THE GAME

Tom Taylor
Writer

Jheremy Raapack
Mike S. Miller
Bruno Redondo
Axel Gimenez
David Yardin
Tom Derenick
Marc Deering
Diana Egea
Artists

Andrew Elder
Alejandro Sanchez
David Yardin
David López and Santi Casas
of Ikari Studio
Colorists

Wes Abbott
Letterer

SUPERMAN Created by
JERRY SIEGEL and JOE SHUSTER.
By Special Arrangement
with the Jerry Siegel Family.

BASED ON THE VIDEOGAME
INJUSTICE: GODS AMONG US

Jim Chadwick Editor – Original Series
Sarah Gaydos Sarah Litt Assistant Editors – Original Series
Jeb Woodard Group Editor – Collected Editions
Rachel Pinnelas Editor – Collected Edition
Steve Cook Design Director – Books
Louis Prandi Publication Design

Bob Harras Senior VP – Editor-in-Chief, DC Comics

Diane Nelson President
Dan DiDio Publisher
Jim Lee Publisher
Geoff Johns President & Chief Creative Officer
Amit Desai Executive VP – Business & Marketing Strategy,
Direct to Consumer & Global Franchise Management
Sam Ades Senior VP – Direct to Consumer
Bobbie Chase VP – Talent Development
Mark Chiarello Senior VP – Art, Design & Collected Editions
John Cunningham Senior VP – Sales & Trade Marketing
Anne DePies Senior VP – Business Strategy, Finance &
Administration
Don Falletti VP – Manufacturing Operations
Lawrence Ganem VP – Editorial Administration & Talent
Relations
Alison Gill Senior VP – Manufacturing & Operations
Hank Kanalz Senior VP – Editorial Strategy & Administration
Jay Kogan VP – Legal Affairs
Thomas Loftus VP – Business Affairs
Jack Mahan VP – Business Affairs
Nick J. Napolitano VP – Manufacturing Administration
Eddie Scannell VP – Consumer Marketing
Courtney Simmons Senior VP – Publicity &
Communications
Jim (Ski) Sokolowski VP – Comic Book Specialty & Trade
Marketing
Nancy Spears VP – Mass, Book, Digital Sales & Trade
Marketing

INJUSTICE: GODS AMONG US VOLUME 1
Published by DC Comics. Cover and compilation Copyright © 2013
DC Comics. All Rights Reserved. Originally published in single
magazine form in INJUSTICE: GODS AMONG US 1-6. Copyright
© 2013 DC Comics. All Rights Reserved. All characters, their
distinctive likenesses and related elements featured in this publication
are trademarks of DC Comics. The stories, characters and incidents
featured in this publication are entirely fictional. DC Comics does
not read or accept unsolicited ideas, stories or artwork.

DC Comics, 2900 W. Alameda Avenue, Burbank, CA 91505
Printed by RR Donnelley, Salem, VA, USA. 9/30/16. Fifth Printing.
ISBN: 978-1-4012-4500-9

Library of Congress Cataloging-in-Publication Data

Taylor, Tom, 1978- author.
  Injustice : Gods among us, Volume 1 / Tom Taylor, Jheremy
Raapack, Mike S. Miller.
      pages cm
  "Originally published in single magazine form as INJUSTICE Digital
Chapters 1-18."
   ISBN 978-1-4012-4500-9
1. Graphic novels. I. Raapack, Jheremy, illustrator. II. Miller, Mike S,
illustrator. III. Title. IV. Title: Gods among us, Volume 1.
   PN6727.T293I55 2013
   741.5'973—dc23
                                                       2013021242

PEFC Certified

Printed on paper from
sustainably managed
forests and controlled
sources

PEFC/29-31-75   www.pefc.org

PART ONE

Jheremy Raapack Axel Gimenez Mike S. Miller Pencillers

Jheremy Raapack Marc Deering Mike S. Miller Inkers

Cover Art by Jheremy Raapack & Tony Aviña

PRESENT

GOTHAM HAS FALLEN SILENT.

THE NIGHT IS NO LONGER BROKEN BY THE SOUNDS OF CRIME. CHILDREN ARE NO LONGER WOKEN BY THE SUDDEN CRACK OF A GUNSHOT. THERE ARE NO MORE CRIES IN THE DARKNESS. NO TIRES SCREECH AS WAILING SIRENS CHASE DESPERATE MEN AND WOMEN THROUGH NARROW STREETS.

IN A WAY, IT IS THE GOTHAM I ALWAYS DREAMED OF.

BUT THIS IS NO DREAM.

THIS IS A PERVERSION. THIS IS A NIGHTMARE.

IT IS THE SILENCE OF FEAR.

IT IS A SILENCE ONLY BROKEN BY THE SOUND OF MARCHING FEET. A SOUND THAT ECHOES AROUND THE WORLD.

OUR WORLD IS NOW RULED BY THE IRON FIST--

MARCHING FEET. THE RHYTHM OF DICTATORS.

--OF A MAN OF STEEL.

I'M GLAD OUR *FETUS* HAS A *HIGH SCHOOL* ALREADY, BUT I NEED YOU TO SLOW DOWN THAT SUPER-SPEED BRAIN.

LET'S JUST ENJOY THIS MOMENT.

BZZZT

IT'S THE PLANET. AN ANONYMOUS TIP. COUNCILMAN IVES IS TAKING A PAY OFF AT THE DOCKS TONIGHT.

I SHOULD COME WITH YOU.

OH, SHOULD YOU? I DON'T REMEMBER YOU BEING SO PROTECTIVE BEFORE YOU FOUND OUT I WAS PREGNANT.

MAYBE YOU ONLY CARE ABOUT THE BABY.

AH-HA! YOUR PLAN IS FINALLY APPARENT, ALIEN. YOU HAVE COME TO THIS PLANET ONLY TO BREED!

AND YOU HAVE CHOSEN EARTH'S MOST BEAUTIFUL WOMAN FOR YOUR NEFARIOUS ALIEN SCHEMES.

CLARK, I'M NOT SPENDING NINE MONTHS SITTING ON THE COUCH GETTING FAT WHILE YOU GO OUT AND FIGHT DEATH RAYS. THAT'S NOT HOW I OPERATE.

I'LL WORRY.

I KNOW.

IF ONLY THERE WAS SOME WAY YOU COULD KEEP AN EYE ON ME AT ALL TIMES. IF ONLY YOU HAD SOME SORT OF INCREDIBLE X-RAY VISION COMBINED WITH TELESCOPIC VISION AND... WAIT A MINUTE.

WHAT IS IT? TROUBLE?

I'M NOT SURE. MAYBE.

THEN WE BOTH HAVE SOMEWHERE TO BE. DON'T WORRY. JIMMY WILL BE WITH ME. I NEED A PHOTO OF THE HANDOVER.

GO. SAVE THE WORLD.

I HAVE NEWS.

LOIS IS PREGNANT.

HOW DID YOU--?

YOU'RE SWEATING, YOUR PUPILS ARE DILATED AND YOUR LEFT HAND IS SHAKING. YOU DON'T USUALLY SHOW ANY OUTWARD SIGNS OF STRESS OR FEAR. THE LAST TIME I SAW YOU THIS AFRAID, YOU WERE FACING DOOMSDAY.

AND I DOUBT IT'S DOOMSDAY--

--YOU'RE GRINNING LIKE AN IDIOT.

JIMMY.

STAR LABS.

EVERYONE ELSE, REPORT IN AS SOON AS YOU REACH METROPOLIS. SHARE ANYTHING YOU--

YOU HAVE TO SEE SOMETHING.

SORRY. I KNOW CARRYING YOU IS A BIT...AWKWARD BUT IT REALLY IS THE QUICKEST WAY.

JUST GO FAST ENOUGH THAT NO ONE CAN SEE US.

I FIGURE THIS COULD BE RELATED.

STAR LABS?

AND WHAT LOOKS TO BE ANOTHER ONE OF YOURS IN METROPOLIS.

YES. IT'S CRANE.

IT'S THE SCARECROW.

I'M AT THE DOCKS. WE GOT LUCKY.

AS SOON AS I SHOWED UP, SOMEONE RAN.

AND?

TELL HIM.

JOKER'S NOT IN METROPOLIS. HIM AND THAT CLOWN LADY HIJACKED A SUBMARINE.

I SEE IT.

LOIS!

WHAT DID THEY DO TO...?

WHAT'S...?

PSSSSSH

I...

SOMETHING WRONG, SUPES?

YEAH, FOR A MAN OF STEEL, YOU LOOK KINDA WOBBLY.

SUUUUU-PAH-- MAAAN.

NO.

PART TWO

Mike S. Miller Bruno Redondo Artists

Cover Art by Jheremy Raapack & Andrew Elder

THE COPS ON THE RADIO SAID MY PUDDIN' IS DEAD.

UNIT SEVENTY-ONE, I REPEAT, DO NOT PROCEED TO ARKHAM ASYLUM WITH PRISONER HARLEY QUINN.

QUINZEL

WE BELIEVE SUPERMAN MAY TRY TO KIL--ZZZZ!

BLAM BLAM

STUPID RADIO.

SKREEEEE

THE GRIN THAT COULD LIGHT UP A ROOM IS GONE.

HSSSSSS

DUMB JOE'S NOVELTY JOKES

I'LL NEVER AGAIN SEE THAT CHILDLIKE GLEE HE COULDN'T CONTAIN WHEN HE GOT ALL STABBY.

I HAVE TO GO OUT. DON'T TRY TO ESCAPE. IF YOU HAVE A FAKE HAND TO SLIP OUT OF THOSE CUFFS OR SOMETHING, JUST LEAVE IT.

BELIEVE ME, THERE IS NOWHERE SAFER THAN HERE.

A FAKE HAND? WHY WOULD I HAVE A FAKE HAND? I HAVE A FAKE MOUSTACHE.

WHY?

NO ONE SHOULD *EVER* HAVE TO JUSTIFY A FAKE MOUSTACHE.

THE FAKE HAND WAS ALWAYS MISTER J'S GAG.

HAVE YOU EVER LOVED SOMEONE YOU KNEW WAS WRONG FOR YOU?

SOMEONE WHO *HURT YOU* OVER AND OVER AGAIN AND HURT THOSE AROUND YOU BUT YOU COULD FORGIVE THEM BECAUSE LOSING THEM WOULD HURT EVEN MORE?

I...

I KNOW HE WAS A BAD GUY...

GENOCIDAL PSYCHOPATH.

...BUT HE WAS MINE.

...ACTUALLY, YOU'VE JUST DESCRIBED THREE OF THE LAST FOUR WOMEN I'VE BEEN WITH.

BEFORE YOU LEAVE, COULD YOU DO SOMETHING FOR ME?

WHAT?

COULD YA GIVE US A LITTLE MANIACAL LAUGH?

NO.

PLEASE. JUST A GIGGLE?

NO!

OKAY.

=SIGH=

HA

THANK YOU.

DRONE COMMAND,
NEVADA

THERMAL
CONFIRMED.
TARGET IS
STATIC.

"ARMING
MISSILE."

CLICK

MISSILE
AWAY.

CAN YOU CONFIRM TARGET DESTROYED?

I...

WHAT?

THE MISSILE DIDN'T HIT.

DIDN'T HIT THE TARGET?

UM... DIDN'T HIT THE *GROUND*.

HOW IS THAT *POSSIBLE*?

I DON'T KNOW, SIR. MAYBE THE TARGETING SYSTEM MALFUNCTIONED AND--

UNLESS *GRAVITY* MALFUNCTIONED, THE MISSILE HAS TO BE ON THE GROUND.

GIVE ME EYES. BRING UP ALL THE CAMERAS!

YES, SIR!

OH... %#--

AND THE TARGET OF THE DRONE STRIKE?

A MINOR REBEL LEADER.

ESTIMATED CASUALTIES?

ACCEPTABLE. BETWEEN FIVE TO TEN CIVILIANS.

IT LOOKS TO ME LIKE HE WAS TRYING TO PREVENT THE DEATH OF INNOCENTS.

HE HAS ALREADY *MURDERED* ON OUR SOIL WITHOUT PUNISHMENT. AND WE HAVE NO IDEA HOW HIS BLUNDERING ACTIONS IN BIALYA MAY DESTABILIZE OUR EFFORTS IN THE REGION.

WHAT HE WAS DOING WAS ACTING AGAINST THE UNITED STATES MILITARY. WHAT HE WAS DOING WAS COMMITTING *TREASON!*

SIR, SUPERMAN HAS DECIDED TO POLICE THE ENTIRE WORLD. HE HAS ALREADY TOPPLED ONE GOVERNMENT. IF HE IS ALLOWED TO CONTINUE, UNCHECKED, *UNCONTROLLED* LIKE THIS...

WHAT DO YOU PROPOSE?

"HAVE YOU THOUGHT ABOUT THE CONSEQUENCES, GENERAL? IF WE MOVE AGAINST HIM AND *FAIL...*?"

"WE HAVE ONE CHANCE AT THIS. WE HAVE ONE CARD WE CAN PLAY."

"THERE WILL BE ABSOLUTELY NO SIGN OF YOUR INVOLVEMENT IN THIS, SIR. THESE WILL BE INDEPENDENT CONTRACTORS HIRED THROUGH A SERIES OF SHELL COMPANIES.

"AND WE WON'T FAIL. WE'VE PLANNED THIS."

"PLANNED *WHAT?* WHAT POSSIBLE PLAN COULD YOU HAVE TO TAKE OUT *SUPERMAN?*"

"I'M NOT SUGGESTING WE TAKE OUT *SUPERMAN.*"

CRRRACK

MOM!

WH OOM

DAD!

THEY'RE NOT HERE.

WHAT?

IF YOU'VE HURT THEM, I'LL--

YOU'LL WHAT? PUT YOUR FIST THROUGH MY CHEST?

SERIOUSLY, THAT WAS SOME PRETTY DARK STUFF.

THE JUSTICE LEAGUE WATCHTOWER

NO ONE STANDING HERE TODAY WAS UNTOUCHED BY THE TRAGEDY THAT TOOK PLACE LAST WEEK. EVERY ONE OF US LOST FRIENDS AND LOVED ONES IN METROPOLIS.

THERE ARE HEROES WHO SHOULD BE STANDING WITH US HERE TODAY WHO WE WILL NEVER SEE AGAIN.

"THANK YOU ALL FOR COMING."

SUPERMAN HAS NOT BEEN MOURNING. HE HAS BEEN FIGHTING. HE TOOK A TRAGEDY AND BEGAN TO ACT TO MAKE SURE IT COULD NEVER HAPPEN AGAIN.

LAST NIGHT, IN RESPONSE TO SUPERMAN'S RECENT ACTIONS--

--HIS PARENTS WERE TAKEN FROM THEIR HOME.

THEY WILL APPARENTLY BE KILLED IF SUPERMAN CONTINUES TO GET IN THE WAY OF GOVERNMENTS.

WHOEVER DID THIS WANTS US TO KNOW OUR PLACE.

I AM PRINCESS DIANA OF THEMYSCIRA AND I KNOW MY PLACE.

"CENTRAL CITY."

WHERE--

--IS--

--HE?

WHERE'S MIRROR MASTER?

TELL ME!!

OKAY. OKAY! CALM DOWN!

SERIOUSLY, YOU LOSE *ONE CITY* AND SUDDENLY YOU'RE ALL HARD-ASSES.

HE'S PROBABLY IN THE BAR.

WHAT BAR?

"WORLD'S END" IN KEYSTONE CITY.

HEY, DO WHAT YOU HAVE TO WITH MIRROR MASTER BUT GO EASY ON THE REST OF 'EM, YEAH?

"HEROES WEREN'T THE ONLY ONES LOST IN METROPOLIS, YOU KNOW?"

FLASH, FER SUCH A FAST ONE, YE SURE DO LOOK SLOW SOMETIMES.

WELL, LOOKS CAN BE DECEIVING.

YOU OF ALL PEOPLE SHOULD KNOW THIS.

AGHH!

NAAARGH!

THERE'S NO DIMENSION WHERE YOU CAN HIDE FROM ME.

YOU CAN'T ESCAPE THIS LASSO, NOT EVEN INTO A REFLECTION. WHAT HAPPENS IF I SMASH THIS MIRROR WITH HALF OF YOU STILL IN IT?

AK!

YE WOULDN'T.

DON'T TEST ME THIS WEEK.

BOLIVIA. THEY'RE IN BOLIVIA! SALAR DE UYUNI!

SUPERMAN. WE'VE LOCATED THEM. SALAR DE UYUNI. I'LL MEET YOU THERE.

TAKE OFF YOUR CLOTHES.

SALAR DE UYUNI, BOLIVIA. MORE THAN FOUR SQUARE MILES OF SALT FLATS.

THE LARGEST NATURAL MIRROR IN THE WORLD.

HERE. FROM MIRROR MASTER'S SUIT. YOU CAN WEAR IT TO ENTER THE REFLECTION.

THANK YOU, BARRY.

WHERE ARE THEY?

I DON'T KNOW. IT'S THE PERFECT HIDING PLACE. IT'S TEN SQUARE KILOMETERS OF ENDLESS REFLECTED SKY.

BUT IT'S OKAY, YOU'LL FIND THEM--

--YOU'RE SUPERMAN.

GO GET THEM.

"SIR, I'M SORRY.

"IT APPEARS THE PLAN HAS FAILED."

THE "ONE CARD WE CAN PLAY" FAILED?

YES.

FIND US ANOTHER CARD, GENERAL--ONE WE CAN PLAY AGAINST AN EVEN *ANGRIER* SUPERMAN.

THAT WAS INCREDIBLY STUPID.

WHAT??

MMMPH!

YOU DON'T TOUCH A MAN'S PARENTS.

DON'T CALL OUT.

THEY SAID IT COULDN'T BE TRACKED BACK TO ME.

IT COULDN'T. I WAS PLAYING A HUNCH.

IT'S NOT A HUNCH ANYMORE, THOUGH.

WILL YOU TELL THEM OF MY INVOLVEMENT?

NO. BUT IF THEY DO WORK IT OUT...

WHAT? THEY WOULDN'T DARE TOUCH ME. THE PUBLIC PERCEPTION--

ARE YOU REALLY THAT NAÏVE? THINK ABOUT WHO YOU'RE DEALING WITH!

NO ONE WOULD KNOW THEY'VE TOUCHED YOU. THERE'D BE NO EVIDENCE. YOU'D JUST GO MISSING.

THE POLICE WOULDN'T THINK TO LOOK FOR YOUR BODY ON SATURN!

SHE IS A WARRIOR BORN.

SHE WAS RAISED AND TRAINED FOR THE FIELD OF BATTLE.

SHE LEFT HER ISLAND ON A MISSION OF PEACE.

SHE DOES NOT LOOK PEACEFUL.

I ADMIRE SO MUCH IN THE PRINCESS.

HER ABILITY. HER POWER.

HER FEROCITY.

SUPERMAN, I HAD TO MAKE AN EXAMPLE OF A FEW, BUT THE REST OF THE FIGHTERS ARE RETREATING BACK OVER THE BORDER INTO QURAC.

UNDERSTOOD. I'LL PROTECT THE CITY UNTIL I'M SURE THE SHELLING HAS STOPPED, AND THEN I'LL JOIN YOU.

UNF!

DIANA!

IT'S ALL RIGHT. IT'S NOTHING.

JUST A FEW TANKS.

DESPITE HER DESIRE FOR PEACE, SHE REVELS IN WAR.

KRODOOOOOMM

I KNOW--

--I KNOW WAR.

DID YOU JUST HEADBUTT A TANK?

ARES!

SOMETIMES PEACE NEEDS TO BE FOUGHT FOR.

OF COURSE.

THOOOM

YOU LEFT THEMYSCIRA AS AN AMBASSADOR FOR PEACE AND NOW YOU *HEADBUTT* TANKS?

WHAT DO YOU WANT HERE, GOD OF WAR?

FOR NOW, I JUST WANT TO WATCH YOU WORK.

I HAVE SEEN EVERY WAR THAT HAS TAKEN PLACE ON THIS PLANET BUT WATCHING SUPERHUMANS WAR WITH HUMAN ARMIES... WELL, THAT'S SOMETHING TRULY SPECIAL.

I AM NOT AT *WAR* WITH QURAC.

QURAC HAS IGNORED THE REQUEST FOR A CEASEFIRE. IT CONTINUES TO BOMBARD NEIGHBORING JUSDAL DESPITE THE COUNTRY BEING LARGELY DEFENSELESS.

WE ARE SIMPLY STOPPING THIS BOMBARDMENT.

CRRSCH

ONCE THE SHELLING HAS STOPPED, THE CONFLICT WILL END AS ALL CONFLICTS DO-- WITH A CONVERSATION.

YOU FIGHT BESIDE THE SUPERMAN.

YOU BELIEVE IN HIS CAUSE?

I DO.

WILL YOU TAKE HER PLACE?

WILL YOU LIE IN HIS BED?

LOIS WAS AN INCREDIBLE WOMAN.

THAT DOES NOT ANSWER MY QUESTION.

I WILL LET HIM GRIEVE.

AND THEN?

HE IS THE GREATEST MAN I HAVE EVER KNOWN.

I WILL BE WHATEVER HE NEEDS ME TO BE.

YOU FEAR THIS UNION, DON'T YOU?

WHY ELSE WOULD YOU BE TAKING SUCH AN INTEREST?

YOU'RE RIGHT TO FEAR. YOU FEAR SUPERMAN BECAUSE YOU BELIEVE HE COULD SUCCEED. WHAT BECOMES OF THE GOD OF WAR IN A WORLD WITHOUT CONFLICT?

MAYBE YOU COULD BECOME THE GOD OF SOMETHING ELSE? SOMETHING LESS VIOLENT.

SAY IT WITH ME. 'I AM THE DREADED ARES, GOD OF PONIES!'

BE MINDFUL HOW YOU SPEAK TO ME.

YOU KNOW I PREFER WORDS OVER VIOLENCE, SO I WILL ASK YOU TO TAKE YOUR HAND OFF ME IF YOU WANT TO KEEP IT.

IF YOU SEEK THIS UNION, IT WOULD BE SAFER TO KILL YOU NOW.

YOU CAN'T THREATEN ME, DAUGHTER OF THEMYSCIRA. LOOK AROUND YOU. LOOK AT THIS DESTRUCTION. I AM FUELED BY THIS.

HNGH.

IT WILL BE EASY. ZEUS HIMSELF COULD NOT STAND AGAINST ME HERE. I AM AS POWERFUL IN THIS PLACE AS I HAVE EVER--

YOU DARE!

THOOM

HOW...?

NARGH!

ON THE DAY YOUR CHILDREN ARE BORN, AMAZON, I WILL BE THERE TO STOP THEM TAKING THEIR FIRST BREATH.

YOU CAN HAVE YOUR HAND BACK WHEN YOU CAN BE TRUSTED WITH IT.

YOU ACCUSED ME OF BEING TOO MERCIFUL, ARES.

SHHNK

ARGHH!!

DIANA!

IT'S OKAY, SUPERMAN. GODS DON'T DIE SO EASILY.

THEY DON'T DIE. BUT THEY DO FADE.

COME. LET US SPEAK TO THE QURAC GOVERNMENT ABOUT A LASTING PEACE. LET US ENSURE THIS WAR GOD FADES.

DO GODS FEEL PAIN?

NOT AS MORTALS DO. BUT YOU PIN A GOD TO THE GROUND BY DRIVING A SWORD THROUGH HIS SPINAL COLUMN AND I IMAGINE IT STINGS A BIT.

...HIS. THIS IS WHY I FEAR THE AMAZON AND THE SUPERMAN TOGETHER.

HE COULD NOT DO THIS ALONE. BUT THE PRINCESS DOES NOT HAVE HIS RESTRAINT.

SHE WILL DO WHAT HE CAN'T.

AND IF SHE TAKES AWAY HIS RESTRAINT...

THE WORLD COULD NOT FIGHT AGAINST THAT.

AND IN A WORLD THAT CANNOT FIGHT, WHAT WOULD I BECOME?

PONIES...

GREEN LANTERN! MOVE THESE SHIPS OUT OF HARM'S WAY.

HAWKGIRL. GET THE PEOPLE OUT OF THE WATER.

SHAZAM--

WONDER WOMAN!

TOOOM

SPLSH

HUURGH!

I DON'T WANT TO FIGHT YOU, ARTHUR. CALL OFF YOUR ARMY.

STAND DOWN. YOU'RE OUTMATCHED.

OUTMATCHED? NO. THE SEA IS DEEP AND FULL OF SECRETS.

WHAT...?

RRMMMMBLE

YOU THINK ONLY THE SURFACE WORLD HAS WEAPONS OF MASS DESTRUCTION?

SHOW ME YOUR HAND.

NO.

DON'T BE *YOU*. SHOW ME.

A HAIRLINE FRACTURE TO YOUR THIRD FINGER. A SMALL AMOUNT OF LIGAMENT DAMAGE. YOU'LL BE OKAY IN THREE-TO-FOUR WEEKS IF YOU CAN STOP YOURSELF FROM PUNCHING THINGS.

DEET DEET

ALERT

WHAT'S THAT?

YOU'RE NOT WEARING YOUR COMMUNICATOR?

NO. I DIDN'T WANT US TO BE INTERRUPTED.

TROUBLE IN THE PACIFIC OCEAN. IT'S ATLANTIS. SEVERAL JUSTICE LEAGUE MEMBERS ARE ON THE SCENE.

WAIT.

I SHOULD GO.

YOU CAN'T PUT YOURSELF ABOVE US, CLARK.

YOU'RE RIGHT. I'M NOT SAYING I'D ACT DIFFERENTLY IF I HAD YOUR ABILITIES. I'M NOT SAYING I WOULDN'T TRY TO IMPOSE PEACE. BUT *YOU*...

WHAT?

THE MEDITERRANEAN SEA.

ATLANTIS.

"AQUAMAN IS SHOWING US HIS STRENGTH."

AGHHH!

TOOOOOOM

"IT'S TIME WE SHOWED HIM OUR STRENGTH."

THE NULLARBOR.

THERE'S NOT MUCH ELSE LIKE IT IN THE WORLD. ONE ROAD IN THE SOUTHERNMOST PART OF AUSTRALIA THAT STRETCHES OVER A THOUSAND MILES OF VIRTUALLY NOTHING.

THE ROAD ITSELF IS ALMOST DESERTED. THERE'S THE OCCASIONAL MAD TOURIST, AND THE MASSIVE ROAD TRAINS THAT HAVE TO CROSS THE COUNTRY THIS WAY, BUT THAT'S IT.

IT'S PERFECT, AND IT GETS BETTER...

ROAD TRAIN

BUT HE WASN'T THAT STRONG.

UNF!

THEY'D DONE A BIT OF GENETIC TWEAKING, SLAPPED SOME TECH ON HIM, PUMPED HIM FULL OF STEROIDS AND TOLD HIM HE WAS STRONG.

AND I COULD SEE IT.

IN THAT INSTANT.

I COULD SEE THIS SCARED KID WHO'D JUST REALIZED THAT HE WASN'T SUPERMAN.

BUT I DIDN'T MOVE.

IN THE TIME BETWEEN EACH VERTEBRAE POPPING, I COULD HAVE ACTED TEN TIMES.

CRCK CRCK

CRCK CRCK

I'M THE FASTEST MAN ALIVE--

--AND I JUST STOOD THERE.

I KNEW HE WAS CRIPPLED BEFORE HIS PAIN RECEPTORS EVEN FELT THE IMPACT.

I SAID, **DISPERSE!**

FLASH, WHERE ARE YOU GOING?

TO GET AN AMBULANCE. DON'T MOVE HIM.

BREAKING UP CIVILIAN PROTESTS NOW? HOW HEROIC.

BATMAN? I THOUGHT YOUR COMMUNICATOR ACCESS WAS REVOKED.

IT WAS. I DESIGNED THE COMMUNICATORS. I UNREVOKED IT.

DON'T WORRY ABOUT THE AMBULANCE. ONE'S ALMOST ON THE SCENE ALREADY. I WANT YOU TO HEAD TO THE ADVANCED SCIENCES AND GENETIC TESTING LABORATORY IN CANBERRA.

WHY?

I COULD TELL YOU, BUT BY THE TIME I GET DONE CONVINCING YOU--AND I **WILL** CONVINCE YOU--YOU COULD ALREADY BE THERE.

OKAY. I'M HERE. WHY AM I HERE?

BECAUSE YOU'RE ON THE WRONG SIDE OF THIS AND I HAVEN'T GIVEN UP ON YOU.

I HEARD YOU WERE COMING. I DIDN'T REALLY BELIEVE IT. IT'S AWESOME TO MEET YOU. I'M DOCTOR NORRIS.

HE SAID YOU WANTED TO KNOW ABOUT THE KID?

THE KID...?

MITCHELL DAVIES, GALAXOR.

GALAXOR?

WHAT DOES 'GALAXOR' MEAN?

I DON'T KNOW. HE MADE IT UP. HE PROBABLY JUST THOUGHT IT SOUNDED COOL. WE DIDN'T EXACTLY CHOOSE HIM FOR HIS CREATIVE SPARK.

WHY DID YOU CHOOSE HIM?

WHY?

HE WAS FIT, HE WAS ABLE, HE DIDN'T ASK TOO MANY QUESTIONS AND, ABOVE ALL, HE WAS WILLING TO DO ANYTHING TO BE A SUPERHERO.

SORRY, HE'S NOT HERE AT THE MOMENT BUT HERE'S THE ROOM HE STAYS IN.

BRACE YOURSELF--

--HE'S A BIT OF A FANBOY.

MITCHELL, ANYONE CAN BE A HERO FLASH

I DON'T REMEMBER THIS PICTURE.

WHY WOULD YOU? YOU'RE THE FLASH. I BET YOU MEET HEAPS OF PEOPLE.

HOW DO YOU THINK HE FELT IN THAT MOMENT, BARRY?

MITCHELL, ANYONE CAN BE A HERO FLASH

I'M THE FLASH--

WHEN HIS IDOLS BROKE HIM?

--NO ONE CAN RUN AWAY AS FAST AS I CAN.

THE RED KANGAROO IS SIX FOOT TALL, AND TWO HUNDRED POUNDS OF MUSCLE.

WHICH MEANS NOTHING TO A TWO-HUNDRED-TO. ROAD TRAIN TRUCK TRAVELLING AT SEVENTY MILES AN HOUR.

THE DRIVER COULDN'T HAVE SLOWED DOWN. AND HE PROBABLY BARELY NOTICED.

BUT I SLOWED DOWN.

I NOTICED.

WHAT THE HELL ARE WE DOING?

CHANNEL TWO. TWIN ANCHORS.

A NATION DIVIDED.

I COULDN'T STAY AWAY.

I TRIED.

BUT THE COIN...

AND NOW WE HAVE TO FIND OUT WHICH ONE OF YOU I'M REPLACING TONIGHT.

NO. PLEASE.

FZZZT

ARE YOU ALL RIGHT?

THANK YOU.

YOU'RE WELCOME. I'M JUST GLAD I WAS NEARBY. NOW, I NEED TO--

HE WAS GOING TO... RIGHT HERE. WITH EVERYONE WATCHING. HE WOULD HAVE...

YES.

WAIT! BEFORE YOU GO. COULD I ASK YOU SOME QUESTIONS?

JULIE. HE SAID HE HAD TO GO.

PLEASE. YOU'RE A JOURNALIST. YOU KNOW HOW IMPORTANT IT IS FOR THE PUBLIC TO BE INFORMED.

WE'VE MET BEFORE, HAVEN'T WE?

YES. WE'VE MET. WELL, I'VE MET CLARK. AT THE PULITZERS. YOU WERE NOMINATED.

YES. I LOST TO MY WIFE.

YOU'RE A WONDERFUL WRITER BUT, I HOPE YOU'LL FORGIVE MY SAYING, LOIS LANE WAS FAR BETTER.

YES, SHE WAS.

GET THE PLANE READY.

THESE TWISTED INDIVIDUALS WHO HAVE HURT YOUR CITY TIME AND TIME AGAIN CANNOT BE ALLOWED TO DO SO ANYMORE.

WHY? WHERE ARE WE GOING?

I WILL NO LONGER ALLOW THEM TO KILL AND MAIM AND TERRORIZE AND THEN BE 'TREATED.'

THE ONUS HAS ALWAYS BEEN ON GETTING THESE PEOPLE THE HELP THEY DESERVE.

THEY DESERVE NOTHING. THEIR ILLNESS CAN NO LONGER BE AN EXCUSE FOR YOUR THREATENED SAFETY.

YOU DESERVE TO KNOW THAT THEY CAN NEVER THREATEN YOU AGAIN.

I KNOW WHY HE'S IN GOTHAM.

ONE OF THESE MADMEN PERMANENTLY SCARRED THIS WORLD.

MYSELF AND MY FELLOW JUSTICE LEAGUE MEMBERS HAVE DECIDED THAT THESE CRIMINALS MUST BE TAKEN AWAY, FAR FROM GOTHAM.

OH MY GOD.

WHAT? WHAT'S HAPPENING?

I PROMISE YOU, THEY WILL NEVER THREATEN YOU AGAIN.

THEY'RE GOING TO ARKHAM!

PSSHH

YOU DO SEE HIS POINT, RIGHT?

YOU KNOW HOW ANNOYING IT IS WHEN YOU DON'T ANSWER?

I MEAN, YOU MAY THINK SILENCE ILLUSTRATES YOUR POINT BUT IT'S ALSO JUST KIND OF DOUCHEY.

YOU WERE NEVER AS STUBBORN AS DAMIAN.

NO. FOR SOMEONE TO BE *THAT* STUBBORN, THEY REALLY HAVE TO BE DIRECTLY RELATED TO YOU.

"BUT BOTH OF US REMEMBER WHAT IT'S LIKE TO BE AN ANGRY TEENAGER."

"YOU UNDERSTAND, DON'T YOU? YOU KNOW WHY WE CAN'T LET THEM DO THIS?"

"OF COURSE. BUT YOU'VE HAD WAY LONGER TO INDOCTRINATE ME."

DICK...

IT'S OKAY, BRUCE. I GET IT.

NOW, LET'S GO DEFEND A BUNCH OF HORRIBLE MURDERERS FROM THE WORLD'S GREATEST HEROES.

ROBIN. WHAT ARE YOU DOING?

WHAT AM I DOING? I'M BRINGING CRIMINALS TO JUSTICE. I'M STANDING WITH SUPERMAN AND CYBORG AND WONDER WOMAN.

LOOK WHO YOU'RE STANDING WITH. KILLER CROC!

AND... UM...

CALENDAR MAN!

HEY, HEY, WONDER WOMAN! DO YOU REMEMBER ME?

LAST EASTER, I WAS TRYING TO STEAL FABERGE EGGS AND YOU BROKE MY COLLARBONE AND PUNCTURED MY LUNG WITH ONE OF MY RIBS.

BEST DATE EVER!

YOU DON'T REMEMBER.

ARE YOU SURE ABOUT THIS?

I'M SURE.

IT WAS ONLY A LITTLE FIRE.

IT WASN'T A *LITTLE* FIRE. IT WAS AN UNCONTROLLABLE BLAZE. I LOST MOST OF THE ARROW CAVE.

YOU'VE GOT TO STOP CALLING IT THAT. IT'S EMBARRASSING.

IT'S NOT ABOUT THE FIRE.

HOW DO YOU EVEN HAVE THAT CAVE AND THE CAR AND STUFF? ARE YOU, LIKE, A REALLY CRAPPY ROBIN HOOD? DO YOU ROB FROM THE RICH AND GIVE TO YOURSELF?

YOU'LL BE SAFE HERE NOW. SUPERMAN LOOKS LIKE HE'S ON THE WAY TO BEING A BENEVOLENT DICTATOR, NOT A MURDERER.

SERIOUSLY. *ANOTHER ONE?* ARE YOU GUYS HAVING A MEETING HERE TODAY OR SOMETHING?

ANOTHER WHAT?

THE PLACE IS FULL OF SUPERHEROES TODAY. LOOK.

LOOK AFTER HER!

SUPERMAN.

HI, KENNETH.

HI, HARLEY. WHY DO YOU HAVE A FAKE MOUSTACHE?

NO ONE SHOULD EVER HAVE TO JUSTIFY A FAKE MOUSTACHE.

OKAY.

TOOOOOMM

P A R T S I X

Mike S. Miller David Yardin Jheremy Raapack Pencillers

Mike S. Miller Jheremy Raapack LeBeau Underwood Jonas Trindade David Yardin Inkers

Cover Art by Mico Suayan & David López and Santi Casas of Ikari Studio

HE WAS JUST TRYING TO HOLD IT TOGETHER.

HIS NAME WAS JOEY GUITON.

HE WAS A MECHANIC A FEW YEARS AGO.

THEN IT ALL FELL APART. HE LOST HIS JOB AFTER THE CRASH. HIS HOUSE NOT MUCH LATER. BUT HE STILL HAD HIS FAMILY...AND HIS PRIDE.

THERE ARE MORE OF THESE SMALL-TIME 'CRIMINALS' NOW. PEOPLE DOING FAR LESS HARM THAN ANY OF THE MANICURED AND SUITED CRIMINALS WHO RUINED THEM.

MEN AND WOMEN WHO LOST EVERYTHING BUT HAD TO FIND SOME WAY TO SURVIVE.

JOEY DIDN'T SURVIVE.

JOEY STEALS...STOLE BAGS AND PURSES. USUALLY FROM CARS.

BUT HE HAD A CODE.

HE'D TAKE ANY MONEY BUT HE'D ALWAYS LEAVE THE CREDIT CARDS AND ID. HE FIGURED NO ONE NEEDED THAT HASSLE.

JOEY WAS ONE OF THE GOOD GUYS.

AND SOME SELF-RIGHTEOUS SCUM JUST SHOT HIM AND LEFT HIM BLEEDING TO DEATH IN AN ALLEY.

SMALL-TIME CRIMINALS ALREADY LIVE IN FEAR. A FEAR OF BEING CAUGHT.

A FEAR OF DISAPPOINTING THEIR FAMILY AND FRIENDS, OR BEING LOCKED AWAY AND NOT GETTING TO SEE THEIR CHILDREN GROW UP.

A FEAR OF LETTING DOWN THOSE WHO DEPEND ON THEM.

BUT NOW IT'S WORSE.

WHEN A GOD-LIKE, SUPERFAST GUY, WHO C... SEE AND HEAR WHAT YOU'RE DOING WHENE... HE WANTS, SUDDENLY DECIDES TO SWOOP ... OF THE SKY AND PUT HIS FIST THROUGH ONE ... THE WORLD'S MOST HIGH-PROFILE CRIMINAL ... WELL, THAT'S THE SORT OF THING THAT C... CAUSE YOUR AVERAGE CRIMINAL TO PAUSE

AND NOW CRIMINALS ARE TURNING UP DEAD--MORE OF THEM EVERY NIGHT.

THE WHOLE WORLD LOOKS UP TO HIM. HE'S SUPPOSED TO BE THE BEST. THE MOST INCORRUPTIBLE. OUR SHINING LIGHT.

AND SOME OF THOSE PEOPLE WHO LOOKED UP TO HIM, THOS... WHO LACK EMPATHY AND DON'... SEE THE HYPOCRISY IN WHAT... THEY'RE DOING, THEY THINK THA... MEANS THEY'RE ENTITLED TO KILL BAD GUYS TOO.

THEY DON'T EVEN KNOW WHAT A BAD GUY IS.

SCREEEEE

AND IT'S ALL SUPERMAN'S FAULT.

AND HE JUST MURDERED A CRIMINAL AND DIDN'T ANSWER FOR IT.

THE GUY WHO OWNS THIS PENTHOUSE TAKES HOUSES AWAY FROM PEOPLE.

AND WHEN THIS BASTARD'S OWN HOUSE FELL--WHEN HIS GREED AND HIS MISMANAGEMENT RUINED HIS COMPANY AND ALL THOSE LIVES-- HE TOOK A PILE OF TAXPAYER BAILOUT MONEY AND GAVE HIMSELF A RAISE.

THIS IS THE TRUE FACE OF EVIL.

I'M TAKING EVERYTHING I CAN CARRY FROM THIS SAFE AND GIVING IT TO JOEY'S FAMILY...

...I MAY KEEP SOME OF THE SHINIER THINGS FOR MYSELF.

I'M NOT ALONE.

CATWOMAN.

SUPERMAN. YOU'VE COME TO HELP?

THANK YOU. THIS BAG IS PRETTY HEAVY.

WHAT...?

WHAT THE HELL IS GOING ON?

DAMN IT!

I'M USED TO PLAYING CAT AND MOUSE WITH BATMAN. BUT WE BOTH PLAY OUR PARTS. WE BOTH KNOW THE RULES.

THIS IS VERY DIFFERENT.

YOU--

BUT IT'S SOMETHING I'VE PREPARED FOR.

WHAT...?

EARRINGS. ONE EMERALD. ONE KRYPTONITE.

BATMAN KEEPS A CHUNK IN THE CAVE. I MANAGED TO STEAL A SMALL SLIVER. IT WASN'T EASY. HE KEEPS IT IN A PRACTICALLY UNBREAKABLE SAFE. I COULD NEVER HAVE BROKEN INTO IT IN A SINGLE NIGHT.

LUCKILY, I'VE SPENT A LOT OF NIGHTS THERE.

MY SUIT ALREADY HAS SOUND DAMPENERS ALL OVER IT. A LOT OF SECURITY SYSTEMS ARE SET OFF BY SOUND NOW. SUPERMAN WON'T BE ABLE TO HEAR MY HEARTBEAT.

I JUST NEED SOMEWHERE TO HIDE. THE SEWERS ARE STILL FULL OF OLD LEAD PIPING. IF I CAN JUST--

AGGHHH!

OW. OW. OW.

FLIP

ALFRED?

BRUCE?

DING

CLICK

HELLO?

ALFRED...?

MISS KYLE!

I'M SORRY, I MUSTN'T HAVE--

OH, ALFRED.

I'LL FETCH SOME TEA. I--

NO. SIT DOWN.

I'LL BE LOOKING AFTER YOU FOR A CHANGE.

I DON'T LIKE SURPRISES, MISTER PRESIDENT.

I'M SORRY. NO ONE HAS SEEN YOU FOR A WEEK. I DIDN'T KNOW HOW ELSE TO REACH YOU.

WE NEED TO TALK.

SO TALK.

NOT OUT HERE AND NOT IN FRONT OF HER.

WHATEVER YOU HAVE TO SAY, YOU CAN SAY IN FRONT OF CATWOMAN. OR WE HAVE NOTHING TO DISCUSS.

SHE'S A CRIMINAL.

ARE YOU TELLING ME THAT EVERY ACTION YOU'VE TAKEN WHILE IN OFFICE HAS BEEN LEGAL?

FOLLOW ME.

I'VE SEEN THE FOOTAGE FROM ARKHAM. I SAW WHAT HAPPENED. I'M SORRY FOR YOUR LOSS.

I'D CHOOSE ANOTHER TOPIC.

"THIS COINCIDED WITH WONDER WOMAN APPEARING IN BURMA--

"--A MASSIVE SHOW OF FORCE FROM GREEN LANTERN AND SHAZAM--

"--IN SYRIA--

"--AND RAVEN SHOWING UP AMONGST THE WARRING NOMADIC TRIBES OF SUDAN...

"...WHERE SHE LITERALLY TERRIFIED THEM INTO SUBMISSION."

YOU KNOW WE CAN'T DO THIS ALONE.

I KNOW. YOU'LL NEED A TEAM. HERE.

WHAT'S THIS?

SUPERHEROES AND OTHER PEOPLE YOU SHOULD CONSIDER FOR YOUR RESISTANCE. STRENGTHS, WEAKNESSES, PSYCHOLOGICAL PROFILES.

NONE OF THEM HAVE ALIGNED THEMSELVES WITH SUPERMAN YET.

WE THINK THERE'S PROBABLY A REASON.

WHO PUT THIS INTEL TOGETHER? LOOK HERE. UNDER PROFILE, SOMEONE HAS WRITTEN 'PROBABLE DADDY ISSUES.'

DOES SHE HAVE ISSUES WITH HER FATHER?

YES. BUT NOWHERE DOES IT MENTION THAT SHE'S ALSO AN ALIEN SPY. THAT'S PRETTY CRUCIAL MISSING INFORMATION, I'D THINK.

I HAVE MY OWN FILES ON THESE PEOPLE.

OF COURSE YOU DO.

YOU TAKE THE WEST COAST. I'LL TAKE THE EAST.

SURE. I CAN'T WAIT TO SHARE THIS WITH HER.

JEFFERSON?

WHAT--?

ZZZT

I'M SORRY. I DIDN'T MEAN TO STARTLE YOU.

SERIOUSLY? THE 'WORLD'S GREATEST DETECTIVE' CAN'T FIND MY DOORBELL?

WHAT ARE YOU WORKING ON?

I'M WORKING WITH THE DEPARTMENT OF HOUSING TO FIND HOMES FOR A HUNDRED THOUSAND PEOPLE EVACUATED FROM AROUND METROPOLIS.

THERE ARE ALSO THOUSANDS OF METROPOLIS RESIDENTS WHO WERE HOLIDAYING AT THE TIME OF THE BOMBING AND HAVE NO CITY TO RETURN TO.

YOU'RE DOING GOOD WORK, JEFFERSON.

I'LL HELP YOU FIND HOMES FOR THESE PEOPLE. BUT I'D LIKE TO TALK TO YOU ABOUT SOMETHING ELSE THAT NEEDS YOUR ATTENTION.

I NEED BLACK LIGHTNING.